20TH CENTURY

Pop Culture

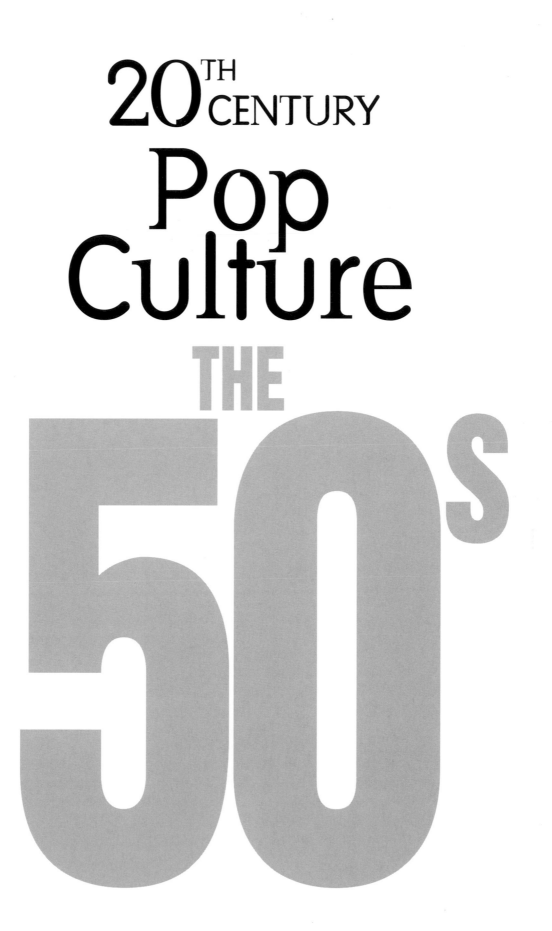

THE 50s

Produced by Carlton Books

20 Mortimer Street

London, W1N 7RD

Text and design copyright © Carlton Books Limited 1999/2000

First published in hardback edition in 2001 by Chelsea House Publishers, a subsidiary of
Haights Cross Communications. Printed and bound in Dubai.

3 5 7 8 6 4 2

The Chelsea House World Wide Web address is http://www.chelseahouse.com

Library of Congress Cataloging-in-Publication Data applied for

The Early Years –1949	ISBN: 0-7910-6084-5
The 50s	ISBN: 0-7910-6085-3
The 60s	ISBN: 0-7910-6086-1
The 70s	ISBN: 0-7910-6087-X
The 80s	ISBN: 0-7910-6088-8
The 90s	ISBN: 0-7910-6089-6

20TH CENTURY

Pop Culture

THE

50s

Dan Epstein

Chelsea House Publishers

Philadelphia

20TH CENTURY

Pop Culture

The Early Years to 1949

The 60s

The 70s

The 80s

The 90s

Contents

50

As 1950 drew to a close, a pall of pessimism settled over the country like a black sheet. The situation in **Korea** seemed to confirm widely held fears that **the Cold War was about to heat up.** Soviet war production was said to far outstrip that of the **United States**, and Americans were getting rather jumpy; one evening in the New York City subway, one thousand riders stampeded when they **mistook a short-circuited signal for an indication that World War Three had started.**

50 US troops embark for Korea.

Movie News

In 1950, the surest way to mark yourself as a Communist sympathizer was to oppose the war in Korea. The *Los Angeles Times*, for instance, advised its readers to report **peace petitioners** to the FBI. "Don't punch him in the nose," the paper warned, "Reds are used to that. Get his name and address and phone the FBI." The *New York Times* also reported that Hollywood's Monogram Studio had shelved a film on the life and exploits of Indian brave Hiawatha, fearing that it might be regarded as Communist propaganda. The studio worried that Hiawatha's efforts as a peacemaker might cause the film to be interpreted as pro-peace, and therefore pro-Communist. However, there was no mistaking the political agenda of Robert Stevenson's *I Married a Communist*, which starred Robert Ryan as a former Communist menaced by his old comrades.

When they weren't busy worrying about the Russians, Americans were loudly venting their disapproval over Ingrid Bergman's decision to have a baby with Italian director Roberto Rossellini—instead of her actual husband, Dr Peter Lindstrom. Never especially adept at distinguishing onscreen life from the real thing, the American public was positively appalled that the angelic star of *Joan of Arc* and *The Bells of St Mary's* could

'50 Gloria Swanson turns on the charm for William Holden in *Sunset Boulevard*.

possibly behave in such a wanton manner. Sparing no amount of hyperbole, Senator Edwin C Johnson of Colorado assailed Bergman as a **"free-love cultist."** *Stromboli*, Bergman's first filmic collaboration with Rossellini, was widely boycotted during its theatrical release.

Far more popular with moviegoers were John Wayne (*Sands of Iwo Jima*, *Rio Grande*), Betty Grable (*Wabash Avenue*, *My Blue Heaven*), and Esther Williams (*Duchess of Idaho*, *Pagan Love Song*). Billy Wilder's humorously creepy *Sunset Boulevard* brought silent-screen beauty Gloria Swanson out of retirement; Walt Disney enchanted viewers with an animated adaptation of *Cinderella*; George Cukor's witty **Adam's Rib** was perhaps the finest ever pairing of Spencer Tracy and Katherine Hepburn; and **Jimmy Stewart** was at his bumbling best as *Harvey*'s rabbit-befriending drunk.

Marilyn Monroe, once again under contract to Fox, scored small roles in *Love Happy*, *A Ticket to Tomahawk*, *The Asphalt Jungle*, *All About Eve*, *Right Cross*, and *The Fireball*. Judy Holliday, perfectly essaying the sort of "dizzy blonde" role that Marilyn would later be typecast as, won an Oscar for *Born Yesterday*. Befitting his method-actor reputation, **Marlon Brando** prepared for his film debut in Stanley Kramer's *The Men*—in which he played an embittered paraplegic— by spending an entire month in a hospital's paraplegic ward.

January 31 – President Truman okays development of the hydrogen bomb, or "superbomb." Many take this as a sign that the US is losing the arms race.

February – Senator Joseph McCarthy begins his anti-Communist crusade.

June 25 – War begins between the Democratic People's Republic of Korea and South Korea. US ground forces land in Korea on July 1.

December 16 – President Truman proclaims a national state of emergency.

Despite all the turmoil overseas, America was doing just fine from a material standpoint. Before the Korean War reared its ugly head, the economy had finally just begun to stabilize; the average industry worker was making $60.53 a week, an all-time high. General Electric boasted that its new automatic dishwasher "will give you over 200 long hours of extra leisure time!" **Betty Crocker**'s *Picture Cook Book* topped the best-seller lists. Diners Club introduced the first plastic credit card, and the US Brewers Foundation wanted to let you know that beer, "America's beverage of moderation," was all right to drink "at mealtime, too!"

Wear To Be Seen

Younger girls were often seen wearing the bizarre combination of dungarees and ballet slippers; slim-figured, "man-tailored" suits and shirts were popular with young women, as were ornate "**circle skirts**," which were usually combined with simple blouses or sweaters. For the first time since before the war, heavy eye-makeup was in.

The "hokey pokey" dance, which involved putting your right foot in, putting your right foot out, putting your right foot in and then shaking it all about, experienced an inexplicable burst of popularity across the country.

Driven To Distraction

Cars in the 1950s differed from their 1940s predecessors in that they often sported tailfins, excessive chrome ornamentation, and two- and three-tone exterior paints. **Color-coordinated** interiors and exteriors, with pastel shades that mirrored the postwar popularity of pastel fabrics in clothing and home furnishings, were a great leap forward from the relative drabness of the previous decade. Car bodies also tended to be longer and lower, as the "fastback" and rounded tops of the 1940s were replaced by flat, "hardtop" shapes. Extra **accessories**—everything from mudflaps to antenna foxtails—became a popular way for drivers to personalize their cars.

As vacationing became a popular pastime for Americans, and the automobile a primary means of vacation transport for the middle class, many manufacturers began naming their cars after popular vacation destinations. Names like the **Riviera**, the **Bel Air**, the **Catalina** and the **Newport** all resulted from this trend.

Bearing the new slogan, "True yesterday—true today," Chrysler debuted its dream-car program with the futuristic Plymouth XX500, built by Ghia in Italy. General Motors, meanwhile, introduced the Buick LeSabre dream-car, aka "the car of the Sixties." The dream-cars never actually went into mass production. For the first time ever, Fords were available with a fully **automatic transmission**, offered optionally as "Ford-O-Matic" or "Merc-O-Matic" (for Mercury).

TV News

Television sets were coming down in price; the no-frills Philco model 1403, with a 12½-inch tube, was available for $199.95. Of course, the big spender could have Admiral's "complete home entertainment" system, which included FM-AM Radio, two-speed phonograph, and "magic mirror" television, in "one luxurious console" and all for the sum of $549.50.

50 Nash cars offered "Hydra-Matic Drive" and "Nash Selecto-Lift Starting."

1950 saw the advent of many television programs which are now regarded as classics. Groucho Marx mixed comedy and quiz show with **You Bet Your Life**. *The George Burns and Gracie Allen Show* and Sid Caesar and Imogene Coca's satirical *Your Show of Shows* are also still fondly remembered, almost fifty years after their initial broadcasts.

Among children, the most popular show by far was the cowboy show **Hopalong Cassidy**, starring William Boyd. Six hundred thousand Hopalong Cassidy lunchboxes were sold in 1950, and everything from Hopalong Cassidy bicycles to "bath roundup" kits were also available for purchase.

Music News

1950 was a less than memorable year for music; about the only interesting aspect of the pop charts was that "The Thing," a trite novelty song, actually charted for three different artists (Phil Harris, Arthur Godfrey, and The Ames Brothers). More interesting musically were the technological developments: the Seeburg company produced the first **jukeboxes** to play 45 rpm singles, and they soon became regular fixtures in bars, bowling alleys and soda shops.

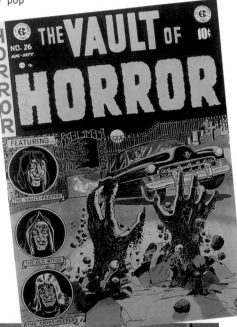

50 "Motor lodges," reflecting the novel combination of driving and leisure, began to spring up all over America in the 1950s.

HOWARD JOHNSON'S
Restaurants Motor Lodges
45 Rockefeller Plaza, New York 20, N. Y.

nineteen

51

As the Korean War dragged on, **America's Communist witch-hunt hysteria shifted into high gear.** The American Committee for Cultural Freedom was founded to "counteract the influence of mendacious Communist propaganda," and film director and "Hollywood Ten" member Edward Dmytryk, released from prison after confessing prior involvement in the Communist Party, became the star witness in the second round of HUAC's Hollywood hearings.

More than three hundred Hollywood personalities were implicated as Communists (usually by colleagues looking to save their own careers), and most of them were blacklisted. Many blacklisted actors and directors retired, looked for work in the theater, or left to find greener pastures in Europe. Some screenwriters, operating under aliases, managed still to find work in Hollywood.

Movie News

With the exception of Gordon Douglas' forgettable *I Was a Communist for the FBI*, Hollywood pretty much avoided the subject altogether, although **sci-fi** releases such as *The Thing from Another World* and *The Day the Earth Stood Still* certainly slipped plenty of pro-peace and anti-nuclear sentiments past the censors. Once again, the year's top stars were John Wayne (*Operation Pacific*, *The Bullfighter and The Lady*, *Flying Leathernecks*) and Betty Grable (*Call Me Mister*, *Meet Me after the Show*), but **Marlon Brando** made the biggest screen impression with his portrayal of Stanley Kowalski in Tennessee Williams' *A Streetcar Named Desire*. Older critics lambasted his method-oriented performance as being from "the torn T-shirt school of acting," but there was no doubt that a major new star had arrived. *Bedtime for Bonzo* pitted future US President **Ronald Reagan** against a precocious chimpanzee. Once a fairly successful B-movie actor, Reagan wasn't getting many parts any more. Despite the commercial success of films such as *A Place in The Sun* (an adaptation of Theodore Dreiser's *An American Tragedy*, starring Montgomery Clift and Elizabeth Taylor) theater owners complained that their audiences were down roughly forty percent. Television, of course, was considered the main culprit.

TV News

Seventeen million Americans now had their own TV sets, and there were plenty of reasons to stay home and watch them. *I Love Lucy*, a sitcom featuring the talents of comedienne Lucille Ball and her Cuban bandleader husband Desi Arnaz, became an immediate hit when it debuted in October. *The Cisco Kid*, starring Duncan Renaldo and Leo Carillo as a pair of wrong-righting desperadoes, was an appealing addition to the TV western genre. Edward R. Murrow's documentary series *See It Now* debuted on CBS, and families regularly gathered around the

51 After a rollercoaster courtship, Frank Sinatra and Ava Gardner marry in November 1951.

set on Monday nights to see the array of amateur and professional performers on *Arthur Godfrey's Talent Scouts*.

The Amos and Andy Show, one of television's more controversial sitcoms, debuted in June; though often vilified for perpetuating racist stereotypes, the show was still the first television series with an all-black cast—and the last one until *Sanford and Son* debuted in 1971. Much whiter was **The Chevy Show**, a twice-a-day, fifteen-minute program starring Dinah Shore. "See the USA in your Chevrolet," she advised, ending each show by blowing a big kiss.

Cruising Stalls

In 1951, American automobiles were still in mid-evolution between the tank-like creations of the 1940s and the rocket-like stylings of the mid- and late 1950s. GM did produce the futuristic XP300 show car for Buick, but the year brought little in the way of innovation—although the 1952 Dodge Coronet Diplomat did feature an "Oriflow system" for smooth rides, and 1952 Chryslers came with "Hydraguide," later known as power steering. Willys-Overland's compact two-door Eagle was extremely practical, but also extremely unpopular—Americans just weren't ready for economy cars.

Pollocks Go On Show

Nor were Americans quite ready for **abstract expressionism**, although

Abstract Painting and Sculpture in America, an exhibition at New York City's Museum of Modern Art, went a long way towards giving the New York-based movement some recognition and respect. Their approaches to painting varied, but Jackson Pollock, Willem de Kooning, Mark Rothko, Clyfford Still, Franz Kline, and Robert Motherwell were all lumped together by art critics of the time; their work did, at least, demonstrate a shared affection for open structures, pure color fields, and anonymous brushstrokes.

Lawn Jockeys Lose Out

In other art news, Don Featherstone designed the first plastic lawn flamingo for Union Products of Leominster, Massachusetts. The hollow, steel-legged bird soon replaced lawn jockeys as the lawn ornament of choice for taste-impaired American homeowners.

Write Stuff

Despite television's popularity, American's still had plenty of time for books. *Kon-Tiki*, Thor Heyerdahl's record of his South Seas expeditions, became a best-seller, as did James Jones' gripping Pearl Harbor tale, *From Here to Eternity*. Rachel Carson published *The Sea Around Us*, a dire warning that effectively kick-started the American ecology movement, and JD Salinger published **The Catcher in the Rye**, his acclaimed novel of alienated youth. Far more readers had eyes for Mickey Spillane's *One Lonely Night*, however; the gritty detective novel, in which Spillane hero Mike Hammer kills "Commies" and gloats about it, sold three million copies.

Music News

Balladeer Tony Bennett had his first big year, topping the charts with "Because Of You" and a smooth reading of Hank Williams' "Cold, Cold Heart." Thanks to "Be My Love," "Because," and "The Loveliest Night Of The Year," Mario Lanza became the most popular operatic tenor since Enrico Caruso. But the biggest buzz in the music (and film) world was about **Frank Sinatra**'s marriage to screen goddess **Ava Gardner**. The couple's tempestuous relationship had been going on for years, but Nancy, Sinatra's first wife, had been unwilling to grant him a divorce. The divorce finally came through on October 31, and Sinatra and Gardner were wed a few days later at a private home in Philadelphia. "Well, we finally made it," Sinatra beamed. Their marriage would last until 1957.

Lasting almost as long on the charts was "Cry," the melodramatic ballad that established Johnny Ray as the closest thing to a rock star in pre-Elvis America; given the hysteria that his concerts created, it's not unreasonable to see him as the missing link between Sinatra and Elvis. The Dominoes created some hysteria of their own with "Sixty Minute Man," an innuendo-laden R&B number that was way too raunchy for most white adult listeners, but which still managed to make the pop Top Twenty. "Rocket 88," considered by many to be the first actual **rock 'n' roll** song, topped the R&B charts in a version by Jackie Brenston and His Delta Cats that also featured a young Ike Turner on piano. Fender Instruments in Fullerton, California, pushed the world one step closer to rock 'n' roll with the introduction of their Precision electric bass.

'51 Gene Kelly and Leslie Caron dance up a storm in *An American in Paris*.

IN THE NEWS

Selective Service Bill lowers draft age to eighteen and a half.

April 5 – In a ruling still disputed nearly fifty years after the fact, civilians Julius and Ethel Rosenberg are sentenced to die for stealing atom-bomb secrets.

April 11 – General Douglas MacArthur dismissed as commander-in-chief of American Army in Korea for publicly challenging President Truman. General MacArthur had advocated attacks on strategic points in Chinese territory, a move that could conceivably have led to World War Three. Back in the States, MacArthur is given a hero's welcome.

American casualties in Korea by the end of 1951: 15,000 dead and 75,000 wounded.

J. D. SALINGER

THE Catcher IN THE Rye

This unusual book may shock you, will make you laugh, and may break your heart—but you will never forget it

'52

Hollywood was in big trouble. **Between 1948 and 1952, television had caused film profits to drop by five hundred million dollars.** Hollywood tried to lure the public back to the theaters with big-budget musicals (*Singin' in the Rain*, *Hans Christian Andersen*), lavish costumers (*Moulin Rouge*, *Ivanhoe*), and slice-of-Tinseltown exposés (*The Bad and the Beautiful*, *The Star*), but folks were much more interested in staying home to watch *I Love Lucy*.

ACADEMY AWARDS

BEST PICTURE

The Greatest Show on Earth
directed by Cecil B De Mille

BEST ACTOR

Gary Cooper

High Noon

BEST ACTRESS

Shirley Booth

Come Back, Little Sheba

Stereoscopic cinema, or "3-D," was mooted as a possible cure to the box-office blahs, but **3-D films** like *Bwana Devil* tended to consist merely of shoddy scripts and lots of gimmicky action (such as spears, knives, and chairs being thrown towards the camera), and audiences quickly tired of the novelty. The 3-D glasses were also uncomfortable to wear, and 3-D's effectiveness depended on the location of your theater seat.

Movie News

Dean Martin and Jerry Lewis were the top marquee attractions of 1952, thanks to *Sailor Beware* and *Jumping Jacks*, and crowds did flock to see Doris Day do her stuff in *The Winning Team* and *April in Paris*. John Wayne played a romantic lead for a change in *The Quiet Man*, Marilyn Monroe played a mentally ill babysitter in *Don't Bother to Knock*, and Marlon Brando played a Mexican revolutionary in *Viva Zapata*. But it was Gary Cooper's turn as an embattled sheriff in **High Noon** that truly deserved the Best

52 Moviegoers wear 3-D glasses to get the full stereoscopic effect.

DEAN **MARTIN** JERRY **LEWIS**

SAILOR BEWARE

HAL WALLIS'
PRODUCTION

CORINNE
CALVET
MARION
MARSHALL
WITH ROBERT STRAUSS

SCREENPLAY BY
Hal Walker · James Allardice & Martin Rackin
John Grant
ADDITIONAL DIALOGUE BY
Elwood Ullman
ADAPTATION BY
From a Play by Kenyon Nicholson & Charles Robinson

A PARAMOUNT PICTURE

Copyright 1952 Paramount Pictures Corporation, Country of Origin U.S.A.

Property of National Screen Service Corp. Licensed for display only in connection with the exhibition of this picture at your theatre. Must be returned immediately thereafter.

52   11

Actor Oscar. Screenwriter Carl Foreman later claimed that his film was an anti-HUAC allegory, but most viewers thought the film was just a really good western.

Hollywood's anti-Communist propaganda reached new levels of camp absurdity with *Seeds of Destruction* and *Red Planet Mars*. In the former, Kent Taylor plays a spy who assumes the identity of a missionary in order to spread Marxist filth in the US; in the latter, Peter Graves and Andrea King play scientists who discover that the planet Mars is actually ruled by God—knowledge that immediately results in the overthrow of the Russian Communist government by religious revolutionaries.

Final Flynn (And Other Exits)

Charlie Chaplin didn't find the "Red scare" so amusing, however. Criticized for never actually becoming an American citizen, the English-born actor was systematically harassed by the FBI and the IRS; having spoken out in defense of Russia during World War Two, he was now accused of being a Communist. While Chaplin traveled to London in 1952, the US Attorney General instructed immigration authorities to revoke Chaplin's re-entry visa until he agreed to allow his "Communist affiliations" to be examined. Refusing to testify before the House Committee on Un-American Activities, Chaplin simply decided to relocate to Switzerland.

In debt and with his popularity severely diminished, Errol Flynn also left the United States in 1952. Though the swashbuckling actor made several films in England, he was sadly unable to turn his career around.

TV News

Over two thousand new TV stations opened across the USA in 1952. Some sixty-five million viewers tuned into network coverage of the presidential conventions in Chicago, but the masses still preferred pure entertainment—it's said that Adlai Stevenson's popularity began to decline after he pre-empted an *I Love Lucy* episode with a campaign speech. Lucy was indeed "Queen of the Screen," but *Dragnet*, starring Jack

Webb as no-nonsense LAPD detective Sergeant Joe Friday, also did very well for itself in its first full season. Fridayisms like "Just the facts, ma'am" quickly became a part of the national vernacular, as did "And away we go," and "How sweet it is" from **The Jackie Gleason Show**. The second half-hour of the Gleason show was usually devoted to *The Honeymooners*, a semi-improvised sketch featuring Gleason as argumentative New York City bus driver Ralph Kramden, and Art Carney as Ed Norton, his dimwitted neighbor. The popular segment was given its own show in 1955.

Mash Hits

Hasbro's Mr Potato Head made television history in 1952 by

52 Mrs Potato Head (*right*) joined her husband in the sixties.

Desert Rats

The Sands Hotel, designed in an abstract modern style by Wayne McAllister, opened on the Las Vegas Strip. A favorite Vegas hangout of Frank Sinatra's, the hotel became synonymous with the "**Rat Pack**," a group of swinging drinking buddies that included Sinatra, Dean Martin, Sammy Davis, Jr, Joey Bishop, and Peter Lawford.

Greenhouse Effects

In New York City, the architectural firm of Skidmore, Owings and Merrill completed the mid-town Lever House; the building's spartan glass and steel

becoming the first children's toy ever to be advertised on TV. Unsurprisingly, the toy—basically just a boxed set of eyes, ears, noses, and mouths that you could stick into a potato—was an instant success. Mr Potato Head finally got his own plastic potato body in 1964, and there was much rejoicing.

Scoring Big-Time

Scrabble, a crossword spelling game invented in 1931, experienced a sudden popular resurgence, selling fifty-eight thousand sets in 1952. College students had other ideas about recreation—on March 21, the country's first official "**panty raid**" took place at the University of Michigan, as six hundred male students stormed a women's dormitory with the intention of stealing any undergarments they could find. The fad quickly caught on across the country, with women students occasionally raiding men's dorms in revenge.

Hat Designers Lose Headroom

As far as outer garments were concerned, the "casual look" was in for both sexes. Men were wearing pinstriped suits and solid-colored shirts without ties, while women preferred tailored suits, long skirts and no hats. The crowns of men's hats were actually growing lower, partially due to increasingly lowered automobile roofs.

Chain Male

Frustrated by the lack of quality lodgings along America's highways, Kemmon Wilson opened the first **Holiday Inn** in 1952. Easily identifiable from the road because of its bright yellow and green sign, the franchise eventually expanded to become the world's largest motel chain.

who had had numerous hits with his wife Mary Ford, and who contributed a great deal to the development of musical technology, the instrument would become one of the most popular rock guitars of all time.

Genius and MADness

Ralph Ellison published *The Invisible Man*, a scathing indictment of racism in America. Kurt Vonnegut published *Player Piano*, his first novel, while John Steinbeck published *East of Eden*.

EC's satirical **MAD** magazine was published for the first time; its avowed intention to make fun of anything and everything made it a must-read for smart-ass high school and college students everywhere. Alfred E Newman, the magazine's moronic-looking mascot, wouldn't be introduced until 1956.

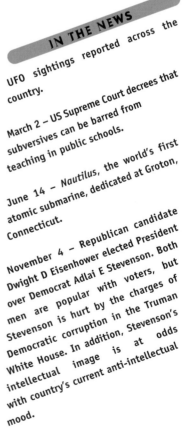

IN THE NEWS

UFO sightings reported across the country.

March 2 – US Supreme Court decrees that subversives can be barred from teaching in public schools.

June 14 – *Nautilus*, the world's first atomic submarine, dedicated at Groton, Connecticut.

November 4 – Republican candidate Dwight D Eisenhower elected President over Democrat Adlai E Stevenson. Both men are popular with voters, but Stevenson is hurt by the charges of Democratic corruption in the Truman White House. In addition, Stevenson's intellectual image is at odds with country's current anti-intellectual mood.

52 Kay Starr gets a kick out of her "Wheel Of Fortune" success.

construction set the standard for office building design in the next decade.

Lincoln Discovers Glass Ceiling

Lincoln slipped plenty of glass and steel into its 1953 XL-500 dream-car, which featured a roof that was made predominantly of glass. But it was Studebaker, a company not usually known for daring designs, who came up with the year's sleekest mass-produced 1953 car—interestingly, it was one of the few 1953 models to sport tailfins.

Music News

1952 was an especially strong year for female vocalists. Eddie Fisher hit the top of the charts with "Wish You Were Here," showbiz vets The Mills Brothers had great success with "The Glow-Worm," and Al Martino scored his first big hit with "Here In My Heart," but Dean Martin's version of "You Belong To Me" was beaten out by Jo Stafford, and none of Frank Sinatra's singles charted higher than number nineteen.

It was a year of ups and downs for **Hank Williams** as well; "Jambalaya (On The Bayou)" gave him his first crossover hit in three years, but he soon found himself fired from Nashville's Grand Ole Opry for "erratic behavior." His divorce from his first wife, Audrey, was quickly followed by his wedding to Billie Jean Jones Eshlimar, a much-hyped event that Hank actually sold tickets to.

The Star's A Guitar

1952 was the year that Gibson introduced its **Les Paul** model electric guitar. Named for the guitarist

The US Government's Small Business Act of 1953 helped small firms and businesses obtain start-up monies; these came in handy, considering that, halfway through the year, a "mild depression" hit the country hard. One business that outlived this recession was **Playboy magazine,** founded in 1953 by Hugh Hefner. Hefner described his target audience as "that select group of urbane fellows who were less concerned with hunting, fishing, and climbing mountains than with good food, drink, proper dress, and the pleasure of female company."

The magazine's first centerfold was a nude photo of Marilyn Monroe, taken during the same 1948 session that yielded her million-selling calendar.

Burger Masters

Urbane fellows (and females) looking for good food and drink had plenty of options in 1953, but those who wanted a quick, cheap burger while on the run didn't have many places to choose from. This would soon change, as **McDonald's** franchises quickly began to spread across the country. The first franchise with golden arches (specifically designed to attract passing motorists) opened in Phoenix, Arizona, in 1953. "Speedee," the original McDonald's mascot, lasted until 1960, when "hamburger-loving clown" Ronald McDonald took over his coveted position.

Dreaming Tires

If you wanted to cruise your local McDonald's in a new car, there were a number of attractive models to choose from. Buicks sported tailfins for the very first time in their existence, the most eye-catching being the chrome fins

'52 Gregory Peck romances Audrey Hepburn on their *Roman Holiday*.

on the 1954 Skylark. Buick's 1954 Skylark dream-car received such rave reviews that the company actually decided to make a limited production version for their customers. Mercury's 1954 XM-800 dream-car was for exhibit only, but there were plenty of auto enthusiasts who coveted its glass-roofed design. Chevrolet's super-sporty 1954 Corvette became the first mass-produced car to utilize a plastic body, and Hudson's small but attractive 1954 Italia was inspired by the increasing popularity of "continental" designs in clothing and automobiles. And, if you could afford to fork over six thousand dollars you could always get your hands on Cadillac's opulent 1954 El Dorado.

Movie News

An unintentional appearance in *Playboy* certainly didn't hurt Marilyn Monroe's popularity, but it was her luminous performances in *Niagara, Gentlemen Prefer Blondes,* and *How to Marry a Millionaire* that really established her as Hollywood's reigning **sex symbol**. The previous title-holder, Ava Gardner, wasn't doing too badly for herself, either, netting an Academy Award nomination for her role in John Ford's *Mogambo*. She also used her influence with Columbia Pictures boss Harry Cohn to help hubby Frank Sinatra land the part of Private Maggio in Columbia's film adaptation of James Jones' **From Here to Eternity**. Sinatra, who had blown his voice out the previous year, was widely considered to be washed up; the role, which he took for a measly eight-thousand-dollar salary, completely turned his career around. Gary Cooper, still riding high off the success of *High Noon*, helped *Blowing Wild* and *Return to Paradise* rack up better box-office notices than they probably deserved. **Audrey Hepburn**'s American screen debut in *Roman Holiday* made a big impression upon American women, many of whom immediately adopted her chic hairstyle.

IN THE NEWS

January – Following a Republican landslide in the November elections, Senator Joseph McCarthy is appointed chairman of the Senate Committee on Government Operations.

March 5 – Joseph Stalin dies of a stroke; Georgi M Malenkov named new Soviet Premier.

June 19 – Spies Julius and Ethel Rosenberg executed.

July 27 – Communist and United Nations delegates sign truce ending the Korean War. 54,246 Americans were killed, 103,284 were wounded and 7,955 reported missing in action.

Summer – Senator McCarthy begins investigating "rumors" of Communist infiltration of the US Army.

'52 A suitably scary poster for *The War of the Worlds,* released in 1953.

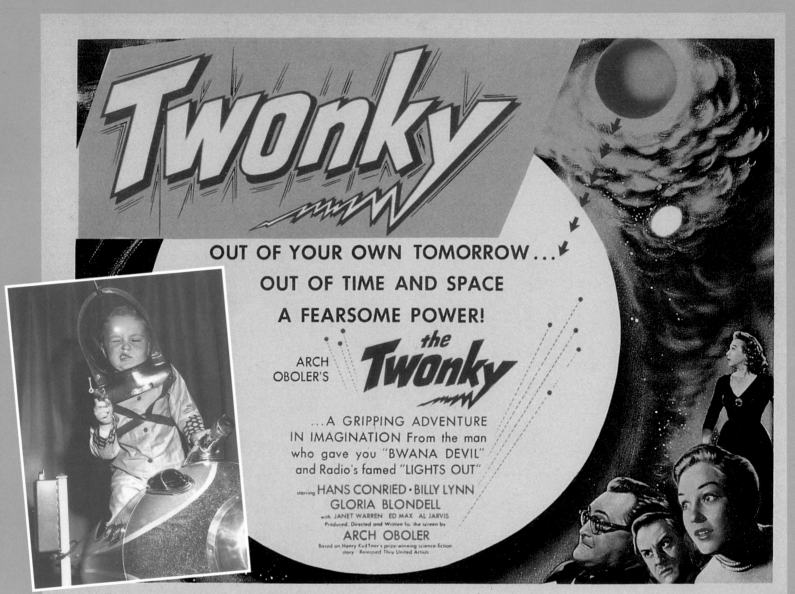

53 At the 1953 American Toy Fair, a young would-be astronaut tests the latest merchandise. The space theme—rocket styling and plenty of chrome—was definitely "in," especially with auto makers.

Overall, it was a pretty good year for films. Fans of lavish costume dramas had Richard Burton and Jean Simmons in *The Robe* (the first film shot using the widescreen **CinemaScope** process), and Marlon Brando and James Mason in *Julius Caesar*. *Calamity Jane*, featuring Doris Day, was one of the year's most popular musicals, and *The Band Wagon* proved that Fred Astaire could still cut a rug with the best of them. *Shane*,

starring Alan Ladd, was easily the year's best western, even if it had taken two years to get it released.

House Of Wax, Vincent Price's first horror film since 1940's *The Invisible Man Returns*, was actually pretty decent for a 3-D feature, as was sci-fi thriller *It Came from Outer Space*. *The Beast from Twenty Thousand Fathoms* beat *Godzilla* to the nuclear-powered punch by a couple of years, and *The War of the Worlds* was a frightening filmic adaptation of HG Wells' Martian invasion tale. The year's oddest sci-fi entry had to be Arch Oboler's *The Twonky*, featuring a TV that came to

life, hypnotized people and tried to take over their lives. Hmmm...

TV News

Goodyear Playhouse, which specialized in top-notch original teleplays, outdid itself on May 24 with a presentation of Paddy Chayefsky's **Marty**. A moving look at two people who find love despite their awkward social skills, the play starred Rod Steiger and Nancy Marchand. Chayefsky later expanded the play into a full-length film, which went on to win the 1956 Academy Award for Best Picture.

Person To Person, hosted by

Edward R Murrow, took the viewing audience into the homes of famous personalities like Harry Truman, Marlon Brando, and Jackie Robinson.

Liberace, the man for whom the word "flamboyant" was practically invented, debuted with his own syndicated show. Enormously popular, the program featured the sequin-garbed pianist bouncing his way through lush arrangements of classical pieces, often assisted by George, his violinist brother.

I Love Lucy continued its reign as the most popular show in America, making television history when Lucy's writers decided to write her actual pregnancy into the scripts. In an age where you couldn't say "pregnant" on TV, and in which married characters had to sleep in separate beds, this was a fairly radical concept. Coincidentally, Lucille Ball's baby was born on January 19, the same day that the "having a baby" episode (filmed two months earlier) ran on national television. The episode was watched by seventy percent of the viewing audience, and the ensuing deluge of publicity completely eclipsed President Eisenhower's inauguration.

Music News

Superficially, it seemed like just another year in pop—perennial favorites like Perry Como, Tony Bennett, Eddie Fisher, Teresa Brewer, Nat "King" Cole, and Patti Page made regular chart-topping appearances, and Les Paul and Mary Ford's "Vaya Con Dios (May God Be With You)" sounded as if it could have been sister to their 1951 smash, "How High The Moon."

But farther down the charts, things were beginning to stir. Eartha Kitt's "Santa Baby" was certainly the sexiest Christmas song anyone had ever heard. More importantly, the healthy sales of The Orioles' "Crying In The Chapel" and Bill Haley and His Comets' "**Crazy, Man, Crazy**" indicated that American listeners were hungering for a greater percentage of R&B in their aural diet.

Take These Chains

One man who would not live to hear these changes occur was Hank Williams. The twenty-nine-year-old Williams died on New Year's Day in the back of his limousine, his body worn down by a steady diet

53 "Long Gone Lonesome Blues"—Hank Williams bowed out in 1953.

of pills and booze. His songs "Your Cheatin' Heart," "Kaw-Liga," and "Take These Chains From My Heart" all topped the country charts after his death.

Ball Park Figures

The New York Yankees defeated the Brooklyn Dodgers in the fiftieth annual World Series, four games to two. The Yankee team, featuring such future Hall of Famers as Mickey Mantle, Yogi Berra, and Whitey Ford, were the first to win five consecutive World Series championships.

Turning Up The Heat

Arthur Miller drew a direct parallel between HUAC's investigations and the Salem witch trials in his new stage play, *The Crucible*.

A Breath of Fresh Air?

Bermuda shorts were the strangest male fashion fad to come along in the 1950s. Businessmen would actually wear the big, baggy shorts to work during the summer months, combining them with suit jackets, dress shirts, ties and knee-length socks for a look that could only be called indescribable.

For all its (not undeserved) reputation as an "idiot box" with no socially redeeming value, television did manage to do something no politician, reporter or movie star had been previously able to accomplish: to demonstrate publicly what a paranoid, power-crazed and utterly unpleasant individual Senator Joseph McCarthy actually was.

'54

nineteen

TOP TELEVISION SHOWS

Between April 22 and June 18, millions of Americans tuned in to watch the Army-McCarthy hearings. For the first time, television viewers got a good look at McCarthy, and most didn't like what they saw—a shrill, tyrannical bully given to statements heavily laden with innuendo and hyperbole; by contrast, Army lawyer Joseph Welch came across as eloquent, even-tempered, and clear-headed.

McCarthy was officially censured by the Senate in December, but by then he had already been publicly discredited. America's fear and distrust of Communism was now permanently ingrained, but at least the witch-hunt was over. McCarthy would spend the next three years drinking himself to death.

Comic Capers

There were plenty of other things to get hysterical about, however. Henry

'54 Appearing on television didn't win anti-Commie Senator Joseph McCarthy any friends.

David Thoreau's *Walden* was banned from libraries across the country for being "downright socialistic," and Frederic Wertham's *Seduction of the Innocent*, a treatise charging that comic books were corrupting the youth of America, became something of a *cause célèbre*. Under pressure from distributors, law-enforcement officials and parental groups, twenty-six comic-book publishers adopted a voluntary code to eliminate obscene, vulgar and horror-oriented comics. Archie, Mickey Mouse, and superhero comics were still deemed acceptable by the new **Comics Code** (even though Wertham's book charged that Batman and Robin were homosexuals), but "all scenes of horror, excessive bloodshed, gory or gruesome crimes, depravity, lust, sadism, and masochism," as well as anything depicting the "walking dead, torture, vampires, ghouls, cannibalism, and werewolfism" were strictly out of the question.

As a result, EC was forced to discontinue its groundbreaking horror titles, as well as *Shock SuspenStories* and *Crime SuspenStories*, the company's two crime titles. EC replaced them with its "New Direction" line, but new titles like *Valor, Piracy,* and *Psychoanalysis* didn't exactly capture the imagination of the comic-buying public. Yet, despite the concerted efforts of Wertham and the Comics Code, the country's levels of crime and juvenile delinquency remained curiously unaffected.

Good Golly!

Music was not without its share of controversy, as well. Due to an uproar over "suggestive lyrics" in R&B songs (Hank Ballard and The Midnighters came under heavy criticism for their singles "Work With Me, Annie" and "Sexy Ways"), various radio stations, jukebox operators and trade papers launched a campaign to stamp out "off-color and offensive" records. Unfortunately for them, American record companies understood that many teenagers preferred the raw, sexually charged sounds of R&B to the sterile blandness of Eddie Fisher and Perry Como, and thus continued to release as many R&B records as possible.

Music News

Thanks in part to the efforts of Cleveland disc jockey and R&B enthusiast Alan Freed, The Crows and The Chords had the year's biggest crossover hits, with "Gee" and "Sh-Boom," respectively; employing a strategy that would become increasingly common over the next few years, white vocal group The Crew-Cuts took a smoothed-over version of "Sh-Boom" to the top of the charts.

Bill Haley and His Comets were the year's top rock 'n' roll combo, riding high with "Shake, Rattle, And Roll" and "Dim, Dim The Lights (I Want Some Atmosphere)." They would soon face some serious competition in the form of Elvis Presley, whose first single, "That's All Right, Mama," was released during the summer on Memphis, Tennessee's Sun Records.

Back in California, the Fender company introduced its new **Stratocaster** guitar, a streamlined electric that would become the preferred weapon of thousands of rock 'n' roll guitarists.

While the young 'uns were busy getting their morals corrupted by that rock 'n' roll jungle beat, America's adults were getting their kicks by doing the **mambo**; the sexual repression of the times found a tailor-made outlet in the slinky Cuban dance.

Dean Martin, Doris Day and Sammy Davis, Jr all scored their biggest hits to date, Dino with "That's Amore," Doris with "Secret Love," and Sammy with "Hey, There." Unfortunately, Sammy's career almost ended in November, when a near-fatal car accident robbed him of his left eye and put him in the hospital for weeks. Frank Sinatra, his voice and confidence sufficiently recovered, had his biggest hit in years with "Young At Heart." He also recorded *Songs For Young Lovers*, the first of many collaborations with arranger/conductor Nelson Riddle, and

54 New York band The Crows flew up the charts in 1954.

his first extended-player for Capitol Records, thus beginning what many consider to be his finest period of work.

Movie News

After only four years in Hollywood, Marlon Brando had taken the place by storm. 1954 saw him play the part of Napoleon in *Désirée*, but it was his roles in *On the Waterfront* and **The Wild One** that cemented his status as the country's new non-conformist icon. Though *On the Waterfront* won him an Oscar, his performance as *The Wild One*'s sullen, leather-jacketed biker leader is the one that remains indelibly stamped on the collective pop cultural memory; replying "Whaddaya got?" to the condescending question "What are you rebelling against?,"

With her bleached-blonde locks and hourglass figure, Marilyn Monroe set the physical standard that all 1950s bombshells would be judged by. In January, she broke the hearts of millions of American males by marrying baseball

ACADEMY AWARDS

BEST PICTURE

On the Waterfront
directed by Elia Kazan

BEST ACTOR

Marlon Brando
On the Waterfront

BEST ACTRESS

Grace Kelly
The Country Girl

54 *The Wild One*—biker Brando stirs up trouble in a small town.

A STAR IS BORN' starring Judy GARLAND and James MASON also starring JACK CARSON · CHARLES BICKFORD with Tom Noonan

WARNER BROS. present Colour by TECHNICOLOR Directed by GEORGE CUKOR Produced by Sidney Luft Musical Direction by Ray Heindorf

Screen Play by MOSS HART These Stills are Copyright. They must NOT be re-sold, traded, given away or publicized They should be returned to Warner Bros. Pictures Ltd., after exhibition.

Cert 'A'

February 2 – Eisenhower announces that the US has detonated its first hydrogen bomb.

March 1 – Five congressmen shot on the floor of the House of Representatives by Puerto Rican nationalists.

April 22 – The nationally televised Army-McCarthy hearings begin.

May 7–8 – The French garrison at Dien Bien Phu falls to Ho Chi Minh and the Viet Minh. Vice-President Richard Nixon urges direct intervention.

May 17 – The Supreme Court's *Brown* v *The Board of Education* decision rules that segregated education is illegal.

great Joe DiMaggio. *River of No Return* and *There's No Business like Show Business* were hardly memorable films, but Marilyn's presence in them virtually assured them of commercial success.

Humphrey Bogart was also the envy of many men, appearing opposite Ava Gardner in *The Barefoot Contessa* and Audrey Hepburn in *Sabrina*; his performance in *The Caine Mutiny* rounded out an extremely successful year. *A Star Is Born* was Judy Garland's first film in four years; the actress, whose career had been plagued during the past decade, gave her finest performance as an up-and-coming singer married to slumping actor James Mason. Stanley Donen's *Seven Brides for Seven Brothers*, starring Howard Keel and Jane Powell, provided rather more wholesome and upbeat fare for musical fans.

There was good stuff out there for

horror and science-fiction fans as well. *Twenty Thousand Leagues Under the Sea*, Walt Disney's CinemaScope adaptation of Jules Verne's submarine adventure, was glorious to look at. And if it took way too long for *The Creature from the Black Lagoon* to emerge from his watery home, his bizarre half man/half-fish appearance (and the film's 3-D effects) made it all worthwhile.

Also filmed in 3-D was Alfred Hitchcock's *Dial M for Murder*, starring

Grace Kelly in the first of her three Hitchcock productions. Kelly also won an Oscar for playing Bing Crosby's put-upon wife in *The Country Girl*, but she's now better remembered for her role as James Stewart's society girlfriend in Alfred Hitchcock's *Rear Window*, which also came out during the year.

54 Monroe and DiMaggio tie the knot.

It was the best of times, it was...well, the best of times. With the Korean War now but a memory, the United States was enjoying unprecedented prosperity and growth. The American steel, lumber and glass industries were thriving, with plastics taking its place beside them as the fourth largest American industry.

TOP TELEVISION SHOWS

I Love Lucy

The Ed Sullivan Show

Disneyland

You Bet Your Life

The Jack Benny Program

TOP ALBUMS

DORIS DAY

Love Me Or Leave Me

soundtrack

SAMMY DAVIS, JR

Starring Sammy Davis, Jr

JACKIE GLEASON

Lonesome Echo

CRAZY OTTO

Crazy Otto

MARIO LANZA

The Student Prince

soundtrack

'55 Thousands of Americans bought one of the new "split-level" houses in 1955.

Thanks to a "**baby boom**," the US population increased by 15.6 million between 1950 and 1955. 1,320,000 new homes were built in 1955, many of them split-level dwellings with habitable basements; the age of the "rec room"—a furnished basement (often with carpeted or linoleum floors) where guests were entertained—had arrived. So had the age of the mall; America's first enclosed **shopping mall**,

where shoppers could visit a variety of stores without ever having to go outside, opened in Appleton, Wisconsin. More and more Americans were installing central air conditioning in their houses, and it seemed as if a new age of convenience, leisure and luxury had come to pass—at least for the white middle and upper classes.

Poodle skirts—full skirts sewn with felt patches of animals, flowers, and

other things—were *de rigeur* in 1955 for fashionable younger girls.

The Happiest Place On Earth

1955's ultimate expression of optimism and wholesomeness was Disneyland, an expansive amusement park built in Anaheim, California, under the auspices of Walt Disney. At a time when the words "amusement park" conjured up images of sleazy

sideshows and rickety roller coasters, Disneyland was a revelation—an immaculate, well-organized "**Magic Kingdom**" staffed by friendly, clean-cut young people. Populated by walking Disney characters like Mickey Mouse and Donald Duck, the park was divided into four themed areas: Frontierland, Adventureland, Fantasyland, and Tomorrowland. Attractions like "Pirates of the Caribbean," "The Haunted Mansion,"

'55 Annette Funicello, Mouseketeer.

IN THE NEWS

January 12 – US Secretary of State John Foster Dulles outlines the government's new "massive retaliation" nuclear policy, which calls for "a great capacity to retaliate instantly by means and at places of our choosing." The great US-Soviet Union arms race heats up even further.

April – Dr Jonas Salk introduces the polio vaccine.

September 24 – President Eisenhower suffers heart attack; recovers.

October 4 – The Brooklyn Dodgers, after years of World Series disappointments, finally beat the New York Yankees for baseball's World Championship.

November 25 – Racial segregation on interstate trains and buses banned by the Interstate Commerce Commission.

December 1 – 42-year-old black woman Rosa Parks arrested after refusing to give up her bus seat to a white man. Montgomery bus boycott begins within days, led by the Rev Dr Martin Luther King, Jr. Originally intended to be for one day only, the boycott continues for over a year, causing the bus company to go broke.

and "Mr Toad's Wild Ride" were designed specifically for the park, utilizing the finest in Disney "audio-animatronic" technology. Southern California's mild climate allowed the park to stay open all year, and "The Happiest Place on Earth" was an immediate hit; over one million visitors passed through Disneyland's entrance portal during its first two months of existence.

TV News

Disney wasn't doing too badly on the television front, either. **The Mickey Mouse Club** debuted in October, and became an immediate hit with the younger audience. The show was hosted by "The Mouseketeers," a group of twenty-four children (including future *Beach Party* babe Annette Funicello (*above*), future *Rifleman* star Johnny Crawford, and future Standells vocalist Dick Dodd) wearing T-shirts and mouse-ear hats. The shows, broadcast every weekday, were divided into five categories: Monday was "Fun with Music Day," Tuesday "Guest Star Day," Wednesday "Anything Can Happen Day," Thursday "Circus Day," and Friday "Talent Round-Up Day."

Disneyland, the company's Wednesday night showcase, struck gold with its **Davy Crockett** episodes, which starred Fess Parker

Sgt. BILKO and Doberman meet Aunt Mary!

as the legendary American pioneer. Almost overnight, the country was seized by Davy Crockett mania; over three hundred Disney-licensed Davy Crockett products (including bubble-gum cards, moccasin kits and "coonskin" caps) were snapped up by consumers, to the tune of three hundred million dollars in sales. "The Ballad Of Davy Crockett," with its indelible refrain of "Davy, Davy Crockett, King of the wild frontier," ruled the airways and jukeboxes in versions by Bill Hayes, Tennessee Ernie Ford, and Parker himself. Disney tried hard to repeat the phenomenon, writing dramas around such historical characters as Texas John Slaughter and General Francis Marion, but had little success; Parker would find further fame in 1964 as TV's *Daniel Boone*.

Honeymoon Season

The *Lawrence Welk Show* was another surprise hit. Debuting as a summer replacement series, the program—essentially a showcase for the "champagne music" of Welk's easy-listening orchestra—wound up hanging around for the next three decades. *The Honeymooners* was not so fortunate, however; given its own time-slot after years as a sketch on *The Jackie Gleason Show*, the sitcom failed to pull in the viewers, and was canceled after only one season. After five years of mildly successful ratings, **The Jack Benny Show** suddenly became one of the most popular shows in America; a mixture of variety show and sitcom, the program's sketches usually revolved around Benny's legendary stinginess and terrible violin playing.

Another popular comedy was *You'll Never Get Rich*, whose title was soon changed to **The Phil Silvers Show**. Silvers (*above*) played Ernie Bilko, a US Army sergeant whose get-rich-quick schemes were inevitably foiled by unforseen circumstances. You could strike an instant fortune on *The $64,000 Question*, just as long as you didn't give an incorrect answer. Hosted by Hal March, the program ushered in the era of big-money quiz shows.

Other new shows included CBS's *Mike Wallace Interviews*, a talk show that established journalist Wallace as a premier TV interrogator; *Gunsmoke*, a long-running TV western starring James Arness as Marshal Matt Dillon; Bob Keeshan's educational *Captain Kangaroo Show*; and *Alfred Hitchcock Presents*, a popular horror-anthology program.

Movie News

Alfred Hitchcock presented two films in 1955, *The Trouble with Harry* and *To Catch a Thief*; the former introduced Shirley MacLaine to the world, while the latter featured **Grace Kelly**, the most popular actress in America, who also received raves for her performance in Mark Robson's Korean War film, *The Bridges at Toko-Ri*. Marilyn Monroe, who divorced Joe DiMaggio during the year, stayed near the top of the popularity polls thanks to Billy Wilder's *The Seven Year Itch*, in which Marilyn very memorably straddled a subway grating while wearing a billowy white dress.

James Stewart was America's most popular actor, with appearances in *The Far Country, Strategic Air Command,* and *The Man from Laramie*. Marlon Brando and Frank Sinatra teamed up for the film

'55 James Dean, *Rebel without a Cause*.

'55 Monroe poses for photographers on the set of *The Seven Year Itch*.

version of the Broadway musical *Guys and Dolls*, and Sinatra received an Oscar nomination for his turn as a junkie in the controversial *The Man with the Golden Arm*. Henry Fonda returned to the screen for the first time since 1949 in the title role of *Mr Roberts*, and Kirk Douglas donned sword and sandals for the title role of *Ulysses*.

Enter Ennui (Exit Jimmy Dean)

One of the brightest, and shortest, Hollywood careers of all time belonged to James Dean, who died in a car crash after starring in *East of Eden*, *Rebel without a Cause*, and *Giant*—the first two of which were released in 1955. Dean remains one of

Hollywood's most enduring icons; his onscreen appearances radiated the same alienation and restlessness that young people in the 1950s (and every subsequent decade) felt, but could not sufficiently articulate.

There was alienation and restlessness to spare in *The Blackboard Jungle*, Richard Brooks'

tough adaptation of Evan Hunter's juvenile delinquency novel. Glenn Ford delivered a top-notch performance as a frustrated high school teacher, and Vic Morrow made a fine debut as an angry student (who smashes his math teacher's jazz 78s!), but it was Bill Haley and His Comets' "(We're Gonna) Rock Around The

SCREEN PLAY BY **RICHARD BROOKS** · BASED ON THE NOVEL BY EVAN HUNTER · DIRECTED BY **RICHARD BROOKS** · PRODUCED BY **PANDRO S. BERMAN**

AN M·G·M PICTURE

COUNTRY OF ORIGIN U. S. A.

Clock," which opened and closed the film, that made the biggest impression on the film's audience.

Out Of The Box

Everything about "(We're Gonna) Rock Around The Clock," from its opening chant of "One, two, three o'clock, four o' clock, ROCK!" to Danny Cedrone's wild guitar solo, seemed to indicate that a new era in music was beginning; the whole thing leaped out of the speakers with the excitement of a school bell announcing the arrival of summer vacation. Self-appointed guardians of public morality roundly denounced

this new music as "immoral" and contributing to juvenile delinquency (a perception that *Blackboard Jungle* did little to alleviate), but the kids were plainly aching for something loud and exciting to call their own. 45 rpm records were outselling 78s for the first time ever, and jukebox operators announced that plays of R&B records were up sixty percent from the previous year, so the timing was perfect for a former country and western artist like Haley to strike gold with a slightly cleaner (but still raucous) variation on the R&B sound. By the end of the year, Haley would earn over five hundred thousand dollars in bookings.

Music News

For the rest of the year, rock 'n' roll records both real (Fats Domino's "Ain't That A Shame," Chuck Berry's "Maybellene") and watered-down (Pat Boone's cover of "Ain't That A Shame," Gale Storm's cover of Domino's "I Hear You Knockin'") jostled for elbow room on the charts with the likes of Perry Como's "Ko Ko Mo (I Love You So)" and Mitch Miller's "The Yellow Rose Of Texas." RCA, sensing which way the winds were turning, snapped up **Elvis Presley**'s Sun Records contract for forty thousand dollars. Elvis had continued to record regularly for Sun, but rockabilly singles like "Baby, Let's Play House" and "Mystery Train" were just too raw to dent the pop charts. In 1956, RCA would change all that...

Recently recovered from a debilitating heroin addiction, Miles Davis blew minds at the Newport Jazz Festival with his performance of "Round Midnight." Counted out by most jazz aficionados, Davis solidified his comeback by forming a mighty quintet with John Coltrane, Red Garland, Paul Chambers and Philly Joe Jones. Charlie Parker was not so lucky; unable to kick his heroin habit, the greatest saxophonist of the era died at age thirty-four.

Frank Sinatra recorded *In the Wee Small Hours*, his first 12-inch long-player for Capitol. Possibly his finest record, its emotional resonance seemed to many to be the result of his recent separation from Ava Gardner.

Falcon Flies

The Fred Gretsch Guitar Company of Brooklyn, New York, did its part for rock 'n' roll by introducing the Gretsch White Falcon, one of the flashiest and most expensive mass-produced electric guitars of all time, with a stunning white semi-hollow body and sparkling gold hardware. The White Falcon was advertised in *Guitars For Moderns*, the 1955 Gretsch catalog, with a list price of six hundred dollars.

Quiet, Sure Pride

The Gretsch White Falcon would have looked lovely perched in the back seat of the 1956 Lincoln Continental Mark II luxury coupe; priced at ten thousand dollars, it was the most expensive American-made car on the market. "Have you felt the quiet, sure pride of arriving in a Lincoln?" asked the company's ads. Lincoln also introduced its 1956 Futura dream-car which, with its bubble cockpit and sweeping tailfins, bore a suspicious resemblance to Batman's Batmobile. Pontiac's 1956 Firebird dream-car, on the other hand, looked more like a fighter plane than an actual automobile.

Indeed, since the advent of Chrysler's "Forward Look" line the year

55 "Don't just play—*do* something!" Bill Haley tells his Comets, rehearsing here at the Dominion Theatre in London.

before, auto makers were bending over backwards to give their products a **futuristic** slant. Ads for the 1956 Plymouth Belvedere praised the car's "youthful, dynamic" qualities, adding that "it has a generous touch of the future!" Chrysler was predicting that, by 1980, there would be electronically guided highway cars for long-distance travel, while the University of Michigan's College of Engineering predicted that electric cars would dominate the market by the year 2000. On a more down-to-earth note, bucket seats were offered for the first time in Chevy Corvettes and Ford Thunderbirds. Volkswagen of America was founded in 1955, but America was not quite ready for the tiny, no-frills VW Beetle.

"I have seen the best minds of my generation destroyed by madness," wrote Allen Ginsberg in *Howl*, the epic 1956 poem that served as the warning shot for the emergence of the beat movement. But most Americans weren't listening; they were more concerned that the minds (and morals) of their younger generation were being corrupted and destroyed by rock 'n' roll.

Elvis Presley, with his pompadour, sideburns, and perpetually swiveling hips, seemed like the most obvious threat to the American way of life, but in truth the music was coming from all corners; blues, country, pop, and gospel singers alike were jumping on **the rock 'n' roll bandwagon**, not just because the music was exciting, but because it sold. In 1956, the average American teenager had more pocket money than ever before (the minimum wage was now a dollar an hour), and the sexy, rebellious music held more than a little allure for those raised in the conservative climate of the Eisenhower era.

Considered a fad the year before, rock 'n' roll had firmly established itself on the charts by 1956, making for a fairly schizophrenic hit parade. Rock 'n' roll singles like Little Richard's "Long Tall Sally," Gene Vincent's "Be-Bop-A-Lula," and Carl Perkins' "Blue Suede Shoes" rubbed shoulders with adult-oriented schmaltz like Andy Williams' "Canadian Sunset" or Kay Starr's considerably un-rock 'n' roll "Rock And Roll Waltz." A few acts, like The Platters and Pat Boone, managed to straddle both camps successfully—the former with soulful ballads like "The Great Pretender", and the latter with covers of Little Richard songs that were as white as his suede buck shoes.

Despite its apparent staying power, there were those who insisted that

56 Beat poet Allen Ginsberg with Lee Forest.

56 Little Richard was a big hit with teenage music lovers in 1956.

rock 'n' roll would soon be supplanted by another form of music. **Calypso**, in fact, was widely touted as rock 'n' roll's successor, which made Harry Belafonte very happy; the calypso craze burned out quickly. The **cha-cha-cha** craze also swept the country during the year.

Pelvis Shakes America

Of course, the year's biggest music news was Elvis Presley. Newly signed to RCA, Presley hit Number One in March with "**Heartbreak Hotel**" and never looked back. By the end of 1956, Elvis had scored ten other Top Twenty hits, topping the charts with four of them ("I Want You, I Need You, I Love You," "Don't Be Cruel," "Hound Dog," and "Love Me Tender"). Not since Frank Sinatra's bobby-soxer days had a performer caused such **hysteria**, and not since Sinatra had a singer split American opinion down generational lines. If you were older, you probably thought Elvis was untalented and obscene. If you were younger, well, Elvis was probably the most exciting thing you'd ever seen or heard.

Most Americans' first glimpse of Elvis came through the magic of television. Manager Colonel Tom Parker astutely figured that his telegenic charge could only benefit from a judicious amount of TV exposure, and while Elvis's first-ever televised appearance—January 29 on *Stage Show*—met with little response, the end of the year saw him commanding a then unheard-of sum of fifty thousand dollars for three appearances on *The Ed Sulllivan*

56 **Elvis rocked to the tune of $50,000 on Ed Sullivan's show.**

Show. Elvis did have to make a few compromises, however; Sullivan's cameras blocked out his "scandalous" pelvic thrusts, and Steve Allen made him dress in tie and tails while singing "Hound Dog" to a nonplused canine.

TV News

In other televised rock 'n' roll news, a young disc jockey named Dick Clark

was hired to host Philadelphia's local teen dance program, **Bandstand**. In a year's time, the show—renamed *American Bandstand*—would be broadcast nationally, becoming the country's most influential music program in the process.

The *Adventures Of Gumby*, Art Clokey's proto-psychedelic series of animated shorts about a flexible green humanoid and Pokey, his orange equine pal, debuted on as

part of *The Howdy Doody Show*. **The Price Is Right**, a game show in which contestants tried to guess the cost of various consumer goods, was also broadcast for the first time.

Ant Man

Despite the evil lure of the rock 'n' roll beat, there were still plenty of wholesome hobbies available to American youngsters, and one of the most popular was ant farming. Invented by California entrepreneur Milton Levine, the transparent, sand-filled **Ant Farm** allowed you to observe the inscrutable doings of a colony of harvester ants. "Watch them dig tunnels! See them build rooms! Marvel as they erect bridges and move mountains before your very eyes!" read the ads. "The Ant Farm is a living TV screen that will keep you interested for hours!" It could be yours for only $1.98. Levine went on to sell over twelve million of them.

Movie News

If you had a movie date in 1956, chances are it would be to a drive-in. Over four thousand drive-in theaters were in operation across the US, an all-time high. Convinced that lavish spectacles would pump up their box-office receipts, Hollywood was producing epics by the dozen (*Around The World in Eighty Days*, *The King and I*, *The Ten Commandments*, *Giant*, and *Friendly Persuasion*), but it also churned out low-budget trash like it was going out of style: if you timed it right, maybe you could catch a double bill of *The Creature Walks Among Us* and *The Mole People*. There were some real gems amid the junk, however; although it boasted both a sensational

sounding title and a star turn by Robby the Robot, Fred McLeod Wilcox's *Forbidden Planet* was actually a successfully ambitious sci-fi update of Shakespeare's *The Tempest*.

Unsurprisingly, rock 'n' roll also got in on the box-office action. Influential DJ **Alan Freed** starred in both *Rock around the Clock* (featuring Bill Haley and His Comets and The Platters), and *Rock Rock Rock* (featuring Chuck Berry and Frankie Lymon), which would be released the following year. **The Girl Can't Help It** flirted with total sensory overload by showing Jayne Mansfield strutting her ample stuff to the sound of Little Richard, Fats Domino, and Gene Vincent and The Blue Caps.

Elvis also starred in his first film, a Civil War drama called *Love Me Tender*. While his notices were generally favorable, he hardly eclipsed the work of his filmic idols, Tony Curtis and James Dean. Dean, in fact, was still the

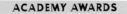

ACADEMY AWARDS

BEST FILM
Around The World in Eighty Days
directed by Michael Anderson

BEST ACTOR
Yul Brynner
The King and I

BEST ACTRESS
Ingrid Bergman
Anastasia

most popular actor in Hollywood. In January, James Dean got 4,038 fan letters, more mail than any other actor on the Warner Bros lot. The fact that he'd been dead for four months didn't seem to make a difference.

Now that Grace Kelly had abandoned the US to marry Prince Ranier of Monaco, Marilyn Monroe was once again the country's most popular actress, and she surprised critics and fans alike with a natural comic turn in *Bus Stop*. Even more surprising was her marriage to playwright Arthur Miller.

Dean Martin and Jerry Lewis's **Hollywood or Bust** should've been titled *Hollywood AND Bust*—hardly able to stand the sight of each other, Martin and Lewis went their separate ways after filming ended.

'56 Yul Brynner, sternly majestic in *The King and I*.

'56 Jayne Mansfield, signed up by 20th Century Fox in 1956.

'57

By 1957, it seemed as if science and technology would soon solve all of our problems. Dr Jonas Salk's vaccine was proving extremely effective in fighting polio, cutting incidences of the dread disease by eighty percent. July 1 marked the beginning of International Geophysical Year, a coordinated study of the Earth's atmosphere, land, oceans, and the Sun by scientists from sixty-seven nations. IGY's first order of business was an experiment studying the effect of the Sun's radiation on communications.

TOP TELEVISION SHOWS

General Electric Theater

Gunsmoke

Wyatt Earp

Alfred Hitchcock Presents

I've Got a Secret

'57 Raymond Burr stares out another witness in *Perry Mason*.

Petrochemical company Monsanto ('Without chemicals, life itself would be impossible!") opened its **House of the Future** attraction at Disneyland. Located in the park's Tomorrowland section (of course!), the pod-like house was constructed entirely from plastic, and was supposed to demonstrate how we all would live in "the future." The house was furnished with numerous "ultramodern" gadgets, including an "ultrasonic" dishwasher and an oven that could be folded away into a kitchen cabinet; forty years on, the only items from the house that have actually become common in American homes are microwave ovens and push-button phones.

Final Frontiers Opened Up

The average American production worker was now making $82.32 a week, and he could easily afford to avail himself of the estimated five thousand new grocery products introduced on supermarket shelves in 1957. These included the technological breakthrough that was Calentano Brothers' Frozen Pizza, the first-ever **frozen pizza** on the market. The Italian pie had been popular in East Coast cities since the early 1900s, but its popularity spread nationwide after World War Two, when GIs returned from the Italian campaign with a taste for the stuff; as a result, the pizza parlor became as integral a part of American life as the hot-dog stand. Thanks to Calentano Brothers, hungry Americans could now enjoy pizza at home with a minimum of inconvenience, and frozen pizza soon became the best-selling item in the frozens aisle.

There was one scientific development which completely rattled the US: the announcement that the Soviet Union had put a **satellite**, *Sputnik I*, into orbit. The USSR was off to a big head start in the space race, a fact made only more painfully obvious a month later, when the Soviets successfully launched *Sputnik II*. From its

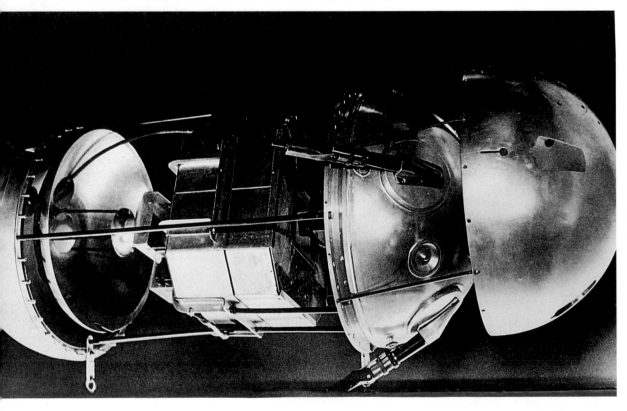

'57 The USSR's *Sputnik I* left the US way behind.

"Oh, Mamma Mia!... wait till you taste Pizza...home made with Hunt's Tomato Paste"

the paste with the Sunny Italian Flavor
Hunt...for the best

extremely well; available for seventy-nine cents, the aerodynamic plastic discs put a new spin on the game of catch.

Music News

Plastic discs of another kind were selling in dizzying numbers, although records by Bill Haley and His Comets were not among them. After a stratospheric 1955, Haley still managed some big hits in 1956 ("See You Later, Alligator," "R-O-C-K"), but by 1957 he had fallen off the charts completely. Some uptight observers cheered this development as evidence of rock 'n' roll's impending demise, but those who

churches to its saloons, America was abuzz with conjecture: Were the Commies spying on us from space? Would they launch a nuclear attack from the Moon? And why hadn't the US, the most technologically advanced nation in the world, been able to get into space before them? Embarrassed US scientists struggled to find answers to these questions, while frantically making plans to send up a satellite of their own.

Latest Disc-overy

Some other interesting items were spotted in American airspace. Originally marketed as "Pluto Platters," Wham-O's **Frisbees** were selling heard (and bought) hits like Buddy Holly and The Crickets' "That'll Be The Day" and "Peggy Sue," Little Richard's "Jenny, Jenny" and "Keep A-Knockin', " or Jerry Lee Lewis's "Great Balls Of Fire" and "Whole Lotta Shakin' Going On" knew differently.

While Elvis and Pat Boone slugged it out for control of the singles charts (with the exception of Elvis, the more adult-oriented LP charts tended to be glutted with film soundtracks and original cast recordings of Broadway shows), numerous new faces appeared on the scene. The Everly Brothers crossed over from the country charts with "Bye Bye Love" and "Wake Up Little Susie," and former gospel star Sam Cooke hit Number One with "You Send Me." The gossamer-voiced Johnny Mathis appealed to more adult tastes with sophisticated ballads like "Chances Are" and "It's Not For Me To Say," but newcomers like Buddy Knox ("Party Doll"), The Del-Vikings ("Come Go With Me"), and The Diamonds ("Little Darlin' ") scored big by aiming their sound directly at teenage ears.

Movie News

Hollywood, correctly ascertaining that teenagers would go see anything

'57 "Great Balls of Fire"—Jerry Lee Lewis.

having to do with rock 'n' roll, also made piles of money by releasing low-budget films spiced up with appearances by rock and R&B performers of the day. Some of these, like *The Big Beat* and *Carnival Rock* (an early low-budget classic by exploitation film-meister Roger Corman), were delightful in spite of their shoddy production values; others, like *Mister Rock and Roll* and the unfortunately titled *Bop Girl Goes Calypso*, were dire in the extreme. *Loving You* and *Jailhouse Rock*, 1957's two Elvis vehicles, were by far the most exciting rock 'n' roll pictures of the year, thanks to decent scripts and plenty

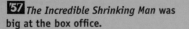
'57 The Incredible Shrinking Man was big at the box office.

of musical numbers showcasing "**The King**" in his prime.

There was plenty of agreeably trashy horror and sci-fi to go around, too. What can one say about a year that followed *I Was a Teenage Werewolf* (starring a young Michael Landon) with *I Was a Teenage Frankenstein*, as well as both *The Amazing Colossal Man* and (the actually quite excellent) *The Incredible Shrinking Man*, other than, "Pass the popcorn"? William Asher's *The Twenty-Seventh Day*, in which an alien space capsule obliterates the USSR, also provided a timely bit of anti-Red wish-fulfillment.

Rock Hudson (*Written on the Wind*, *Battle Hymn*, *Something of Value*, *A Farewell to Arms*) and **Kim Novak**

ACADEMY AWARDS

BEST PICTURE
The Bridge on the River Kwai
directed by David Lean

BEST ACTOR
Alec Guinness
The Bridge on the River Kwai

BEST ACTRESS
Joanne Woodward
The Three Faces of Eve

(*Jeanne Eagels*, *Pal Joey*) were the year's hottest stars, while audiences turned out *en masse* for *Funny Face* (with Audrey Hepburn and Fred Astaire), *Twelve Angry Men* (with Henry Fonda), and, of course, *Peyton Place* (starring Lana Turner). Movie fans everywhere mourned the passing of Humphrey Bogart, who died of cancer of the esophagus at the age of fifty-seven.

Yee-ha!

Gunsmoke had already debuted a few years earlier, but it wasn't until 1957 that the western, a genre slowly dying at the box office, found new life on the small screen. *Have Gun Will Travel*, *Wagon Train*, *The Restless Gun*, *Tales of Wells Fargo*, and *Maverick* all debuted within months of each other, while ratings of older shows like *Cheyenne* and *Wyatt Earp* suddenly rocketed skyward. Though popular with the same younger demographic that fueled the Davy Crockett craze, subtler, more complex characters like *Maverick*'s cowardly title rogue (played by James Garner) were clearly written with an adult audience in mind.

Perry Mason, starring Raymond Burr as a methodical lawyer, was also a big hit with adult viewers.

US Senate subcommittee holds hearings on America's ability to withstand Soviet military attack.

US occupation forces leave Japan.

May 2 – Senator Joseph McCarthy dies of cirrhosis of the liver at age 48.

July 12 – US Surgeon General reports link between cigarette smoking and lung cancer.

September 19 – In the desert outside Las Vegas, the Atomic Energy Commission detonates first underground atomic blast.

September 24 – 1,000 army paratroopers called in by President Eisenhower to ensure the integration of Central High School in Little Rock, Arkansas.

October 4 – Soviet Union launches the first manmade satellite, Sputnik I.

November 3 – Soviet Union launches Sputnik II; canine passenger Laika becomes the first living Earth creature to travel (and die) in outer space.

TV News

In any case, there was plenty of stuff for the kids. *American Bandstand* debuted on ABC, and quickly ignited nationwide dance fads like the bunny hop, the bop, the slop, the pony, the chicken, the monkey, and the stroll. **Leave It to Beaver**, a sitcom revolving around the well-intentioned antics of young "Beaver" Cleaver (played by Jerry Mathers) and his friends, debuted on CBS; reruns of the show would continue to be popular for

decades afterward, partly because of its idyllic depiction of American suburban life in the late fifties and early sixties. And Robert Strom, a ten-year-old science buff, won $192,000 in three rounds of *The $64,000 Question*.

Kennedys Box Clever

No dummies themselves, brothers Robert and John F Kennedy received plenty of valuable exposure through the nationally televised hearings of the Senate Rackets Committee, in which the two Kennedys interrogated numerous known and alleged organized crime figures. JFK was also awarded a Pulitzer Prize for his book, *Profiles in Courage*, which saluted various US senators throughout history who had defied public opinion for the good of the country.

Dr Seuss (aka Theodore Seuss Geisel) published two classic children's books, *The Cat in the Hat* and *The Grinch that Stole Christmas*. **On the Road**, Jack Kerouac's compendium of cross-country musings and adventures, quickly became a must-read for any would-be hipster.

The Edsel Episode

Of course, for most Americans, "on the road" was merely where they drove, showing off their fabulously finned and chromed vehicles as they went to the supermarket, the drive-in or their jobs. Most auto makers were going overboard with their chrome trimmings: heaps of chrome covered the doors, wheel-wells, and hoods, not to mention bumpers, radiator grilles and hood ornaments. Buick reintroduced and updated its "Limited" line from the 1940s, offering the extra-long,

ostentatiously trimmed Riviera coupe, Riviera sedan, and Riviera convertible for five thousand dollars apiece.

Also fabulously chromed, if rather awkwardly shaped, was Ford's 1958 Edsel. While hardly the worst car ever made, the car's over-the-top advance hype, questionable ornamentation (the new-fangled radiator grille was alternately compared to a cattle yoke, a toilet seat, and a vagina), excessive gadgetry (including a "teletouch" transmission and a speedometer that glowed red when the car exceeded a pre-set speed limit), and just plain bad luck (it was introduced in the middle of 1957's recession) ultimately set it up for failure; the fact that many of the early models seemed to experience endless technical difficulties didn't help improve its reputation and, in the minds of the American public, "Edsel" quickly became synonymous with "lemon." Ford tried again in 1958 with a slightly modified design and an understated ad campaign, but they still wound up losing two hundred and fifty million dollars on the car, which was finally discontinued in 1959.

There was a little bit of good news for Ford in 1957, however. The company's new four-door Thunderbird sedan proved far more popular than its previous two-seater incarnation.

'57 Michael Landon in *I Was a Teenage Werewolf*, billed as "The most amazing motion picture of our time!"

nineteen '58

"The New-day woman won't sit still for the filling foods of yesteryear," noted a magazine ad for Pepsi-Cola. "She's thankful for the whole modern trend toward light food and drink. And don't you notice the slim-and-slender difference?" Actually, if your "New-day" woman was looking more "slim and slender" than usual, it might have been because she couldn't afford to eat on a regular basis.

TOP TELEVISION SHOWS

Gunsmoke

Have Gun, Will Travel

The Danny Thomas Show

Tales of Wells Fargo

I've Got a Secret

The 1958 recession was the country's worst since World War Two, and almost five and a half million people were out of work. Not coincidentally, 1958 saw a rise in the sales of lower-priced "convenience foods"—according to one study, over four hundred million frozen pot pies were consumed during the year.

Time For Change

If you could afford new clothes, there were big changes afoot in the fashion world. Floral prints and knee-length skirts were now quite popular with women, as were short-sleeved dresses and "Empire waist" three-quarter coats. False eyelashes became a popular accessory, as did turbans. The bulky men's suits and wide neckties of the last few decades were out, replaced by sleek, narrow-lapelled suits and shiny, narrow ties. Brightly patterned sports shirts were also popular, and were often worn with solid-colored four-button cardigan sweaters.

'58 Winning style: Catalina sweaters for him and her.

California magic in Sweaters

FOR HER: Cable-Knit Coat, 11.00
FOR HIM: Cable-Knit Pullover, 8.50

Catalina
LOOK FOR THE FLYING FISH

Hula-Hype

With hard times at hand, Americans were in need of distraction, and they got it in the circular form of the Hula-Hoop. The toy was brought back from Australia by Richard Knerr and Arthur "Spud" Melin of the Wham-O company, who had experienced great success the previous year with the Frisbee. Introduced in California in the Spring of 1958, the Hula-Hoop (now changed from the wood of the Australian "exercise rings" to light plastic) was a household item across the country by the end of the summer. Priced at $1.98, Wham-O's Hula-Hoop sold over seventy million units, and inspired a legion of imitators, including Spin-A-Hoop, Wiggle-A-Hoop, Hoop-Zing, Hooper Dooper, and Whoop-De-Do.

Spun from around the waist (or, in a popular variation, from around the neck), the Hula-Hoop required some dexterity to use successfully. It also required a fair amount of open space; consequently, when the winter of 1958 commenced, sales of the hoops immediately plummeted. Trying to cash in on the fad, Georgia Gibbs,

Teresa Brewer, and Betty Johnson all recorded Hula-Hoop-themed songs, but the Hula-Hoop craze died out before any of them could become hits.

Board Minds

In Dana Point, California, Bill and Mark Richards invented the first skateboard, attaching wheels from rollerskates to a square wooden board. The Richards sold the boards at their Val Surf Shop for eight dollars apiece.

Nation Tires Of Cruising

The needs of American drivers were changing, and cars were beginning to evolve along with them. Tailfins, now far more of a status symbol than an actual engineering necessity (despite the claims of various manufacturers), were larger and more popular than ever. 1959 Chevrolets and Buicks sported sideways "gull wing" fins, while the huge fins of the 1959 Cadillac were possibly the ultimate in automotive appendages. The "lion-hearted" '59 Chrysler New Yorker came with optional swivel seats (also available on all Plymouths, Dodges, DeSotos, Chryslers, and Imperials), and "Auto-Pilot" (an early version of cruise control), not to mention bold tailfins and expansive safety-glass windshields. Pontiac's "wide-track wheels" were moved five inches out from their previous position "for the widest, steadiest stance in America," while the '59 Oldsmobile's new "**Linear Look**" anticipated the full-sized cars of the next decade with its flat roof and tapered fins.

By 1958, however, many Americans no longer felt the need to impress others with the size of their tailfins, just as many could no longer afford to drive gas-guzzling luxury cars. The 1959 Ranchero was Ford's concession to the need for a more utilitarian vehicle, combining economy-car styling with the loadspace of a pickup truck. AMC's new economy-sized Rambler **compact** proved extremely popular, and Studebaker introduced the Lark, a compact smaller than the Rambler but larger than the VW Bug; "This is your new dimension," bragged Studebaker's ads. Foreign imports still weren't faring too well, though; Chrysler imported the compact Simca from France, but found few takers. Datsun, the first Japanese export available in the US, sold only eighty-three cars in its first year here.

To Rig Or Not To Rig...

Vladimir Nabokov's *Lolita*, the story of an older man's obsession with an underage girl, was 1958's most controversial best-seller, but the year's biggest scandal happened on television, when the game show **Twenty-One** was revealed to be rigged. As dramatized in the 1994 film *Quiz Show*, contestant Charles Van Doren had been given some correct answers in advance by the show's producers, enabling him to win one hundred and twenty-nine thousand dollars in prize money over fourteen appearances; a handsome, articulate English instructor at Columbia University, Van Doren was popular with the viewing audience, and the producers wanted to keep him on as many broadcasts as possible. When contestant Herbert Stempel (who had lost to Van Doren) went public with the truth, the ensuing brouhaha caused not only the cancelation of the program, but the cancelation of game shows *Dotto*, *The $64,000 Question*, and *The $64,000 Challenge*.

TV News

The "adult western" continued to flourish on television, with successful debuts by *The Rifleman*, *The Texan*, and *Wanted—Dead or Alive*. 1958 also witnessed the debut of two popular detective shows, *Peter Gunn*, and **77 Sunset Strip**. The latter starred Efrem Zimbalist, Jr as a Hollywood private eye, but the show's secret

58 Efrem Zimbalist, Jr, Edd Byrnes, and Roger Smith of *77 Sunset Strip*.

School integration debate intensifies in South; many schools close or become privatized in order to avoid having to enroll black students.

January 31 – US launches *Explorer I* satellite into orbit.

March 17 – US launches *Vanguard 1* satellite into orbit; the 6.4-inch aluminum sphere goes into wider orbit than any previous manmade satellite.

July 7 – Alaska statehood bill signed by President Eisenhower.

October 11 – US launches *Pioneer* rocket in attempt to orbit the Moon. Project fails, but rocket does achieve a record altitude of 79,193 miles.

'58 A mystery girl has eyes only for Rick Nelson on the *Ozzie and Harriet* show.

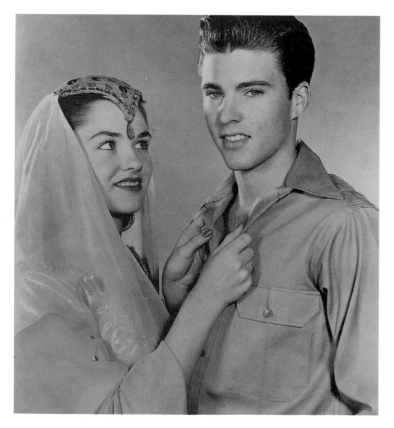

weapon was Kookie, the jive-talking parking lot attendant played by Edd Byrnes. Byrnes later parlayed his character into a briefly successful recording career, hitting biggest with "Kookie, Kookie (Lend Me Your Comb)."

Another TV actor with musical ambitions was **Rick Nelson**, the youngest member of the Nelson family, who played themselves on the long-running show *The Adventures of Ozzie and Harriet*. He performed regularly on the show, fronting a band that included future Elvis sideman James Burton, and had a series of chart hits, including "Be-Bop Baby" and "Poor Little Fool."

Music News

The musical events of 1958 were enough to try the patience of even the most die-hard rock 'n' roll fan. At the peak of his career, Elvis had been drafted into the army; Colonel Tom

'58 Chart-topping teenager Laurie London.

Parker, his manager, thought that it would be better for Elvis's image to serve his allotted two years than to ask for a special dispensation from the draft board. **Jerry Lee Lewis** single-handedly derailed his own career by marrying his thirteen-year-old cousin, Myra Gale Brown; Lewis's concert and TV appearances were canceled as soon as the news slipped out, and "The Killer" became a pariah almost overnight. The country's new piano hero was the considerably more urbane Van Cliburn, the twenty-three-year-old pianist who had just won the international Tchaikovsky competition in Moscow.

Real rockers like Chuck Berry and Buddy Holly were also being crowded off the charts by an endless succession of novelty singles, such as David Seville's "Witch Doctor" and Sheb Wooley's "Purple People Eater," as well as treacly pap like Laurie

London's "He's Got The Whole World In His Hands." When The Kingston Trio had a successful hit with "Tom Dooley," many predicted that folk music would soon displace rock 'n' roll. Perhaps that's why Gibson had a hard time interesting guitarists in its new, futuristically shaped Explorer and Flying V guitars, while the company's semi-hollow ES-335 was an immediate success.

"Rumble," a brooding guitar instrumental by **Link Wray**, was banned in many markets for "encouraging juvenile delinquency," and so enjoyed only moderate chart success. Wray's influence would be felt more heavily in the next decade, when guitarists on both sides of the Atlantic would draw upon his violent, feedback-laced sound to power their hard rock and heavy metal stylings.

Sounds More Like It

With the introduction of the stereophonic LP (RCA, Columbia and Atlantic also began releasing stereo 45s in 1958), "high fidelity" was the big buzzphrase in the music industry.

Consumers investing a bundle in expensive stereo components craved records that could really test (and show off) their stereo's sonic capabilities, and audiophile-oriented records like RCA's *Living Stereo* series were born. The king of "**hi-fi**" was Esquivel, a Mexican composer and conductor whose head-spinning arrangements were written to take utmost advantage of the stereo spectrum. His mastery could be heard on albums like *Other Worlds, Other Sounds*.

Miles Ahead

In New York, Miles Davis formed a sextet with John Coltrane, Cannonball Adderly, Bill Evans, Paul Chambers, and Philly Joe Jones, an aggregation that's still widely considered to be his finest band. Meanwhile, Duke Ellington was the hit of the Newport Jazz Festival, performing excerpts from his jazz suite, *Black, Brown And Beige*.

Movie News

There was still plenty of rock 'n' roll in the theaters, however; Jerry Lee Lewis raised hell on the back of a flatbed truck during the opening sequence of *High School Confidential* (which also starred popular B-movie bombshell Mamie Van Doren), Elvis delivered another respectable performance (this time as a boxer) in *King Creole*, and there was juvenile delinquency to spare in *The Cool and the Crazy*, *Dragstrip Riot*, *Hot Rod Gang*, and *Teenage Thunder*. *The Fly* and **The Seventh Voyage of Sinbad** were some of the year's better horror and adventure titles, respectively; the latter film's memorable "fighting skeletons" sequence still stands as a mighty testament to the mind-boggling abilities of animator Ray Harryhausen.

Look magazine named Rock Hudson its "Star of the Year" for his performances in *The Tarnished Angels* and *Twilight for the Gods*. However, it was Glenn Ford (*Cowboy*, *The Sheepman*, *Imitation General*, and *Torpedo Run*) who really cleaned up at the box office. **Elizabeth Taylor** had her finest role yet, as Maggie in Tennessee Williams' *Cat on a Hot Tin Roof*, but was severely traumatized by the airplane crash death of her third husband, producer Mike Todd.

Other highlights included *The Defiant Ones*, a gripping prison escape film starring Tony Curtis

and Sidney Poitier; *Touch of Evil*, Orson Welles' tale of corruption in a Mexican border town; and *The Young Lions*, Edward Dymytryk's World War Two film starring Marlon Brando, Dean Martin and Montgomery Clift. *Gigi*, starring Leslie Caron, and *Damn Yankees* (featuring the stage standard "Whatever Lola Wants") were the year's top musicals.

Off-Set Upset

Tragedy struck Hollywood on April 4, when Cheryl Crane, Lana Turner's fourteen-year-old daughter, was arrested for the stabbing to death of gangster Johnny Stompanato, Turner's boyfriend. Crane claimed that she heard Stompanato threatening her mother, and the jury ruled it a justifiable homicide. Later in the year, former matinee idol Tyrone Power died of heart attack on the set of *Solomon and Sheba*, a biblical costume epic starring Gina Lollobrigida. He was replaced by Yul Brynner.

58 Hot property—Paul Newman and Elizabeth Taylor in *Cat on a Hot Tin Roof*.

nineteen **'59**

"The new leisure is here," trumpeted *Life* magazine's year-end issue of 1959. "For the first time, a civilization has reached a point where most people are no longer preoccupied with providing food and shelter." The issue went on to note blithely that there were now over two hundred and fifty thousand swimming pools in US homes. Never before had the nation experienced such an overwhelming degree of opulence.

'59 Hawaiian-style leisure wear for less formal times.

Despite a 116-day steelworkers' strike—the longest in US history—the nation's economy was again in good shape, thanks in part to the government's "**Buy American**" campaign. America's aerospace industry was booming as the nation began to challenge Russia's lead in the space race. The average American worker earned $91.53 a week, and was looking for new ways in which to spend it.

This abundance of disposable income, combined with Hawaii's recent entrance into the Union in 1959, manifested itself in a mania for all things Hawaiian. Polynesian restaurant-bars like Don The Beachcomber's and Trader Vic's had been serving mai-tais since before World War Two, but now "tiki" bars (usually furnished with excessive amounts of bamboo and blowfish lanterns) were springing up all over the place. Housewives were taking hula lessons, and suburbanites everywhere were holding weekend luaus in their back yards—which, in turn, were often transformed into miniature tropical paradises replete with palm

trees, tiki torches, and statues of Polynesian gods.

Music News
Despite being stationed in Germany, Elvis was still selling healthy quantities

of records; he had recorded songs like "A Fool Such As I" and "Big Hunk O' Love" before his induction, in order to keep the charts warm until his return. Inferior Elvis substitutes Fabian ("Tiger"), Frankie Avalon ("Venus"), and Bobby Rydell ("We

'59 Khrushchev doffs his hat as Eisenhower welcomes him to the US at Andrews Air Force Base, Maryland.

Got Love") all took advantage of Elvis's absence by ingratiating themselves into the hearts of his teenage fans.

But there were worse things than a missing Elvis to contend with. In February, Buddy Holly, Ritchie Valens, and The Big Bopper all ended their promising careers in a plane crash near Mason City, Iowa. In November, Alan Freed, one of rock 'n' roll's most influential proponents, was forced to resign his DJ post at New York City's WABC. The US government was investigating reports that DJs were accepting monetary bribes in return for airplay, and was only too happy to make Freed the scapegoat of the "**payola**" scandal. Freed received a four-hundred-dollar fine and a suspended jail sentence, and was essentially drummed out of the music business; by 1965, "The Father of Rock 'n' Roll" was dead, the victim of alcoholism and a broken heart.

In what many consider to have been his finest year, Miles Davis completed *Kind Of Blue* and began working on *Sketches Of Spain*. Meanwhile, saxophonist Ornette Coleman recorded *The Shape Of Jazz*, a defining work of "free jazz," with trumpet player Don Cherry, bassist

TOP SINGLES

BOBBY DARIN
"Mack The Knife"

JOHNNY HORTON
"The Battle Of New Orleans"

FRANKIE AVALON
"Venus"

THE FLEETWOODS
"Come Softly To Me"

LLOYD PRICE
"Stagger Lee"

Charlie Haden, and drummer Billy Higgins. Billie Holiday, one of the finest jazz and blues vocalists ever, died broke and addicted at age forty-four.

TV News

Predictably, television also cashed in on the Polynesian craze: *Hawaiian Eye*, a detective show set in

Honolulu, made its debut on ABC, as did *Adventure in Paradise*, about the captain (Gardner McKay) of a South Seas schooner. Other notable debuts included *Bonanza*, a long-running "ranch" western starring Lorne Greene as Pa Cartwright; *The Untouchables*, a crime show set in 1930s Chicago, starring Robert Stack

59 Frankie Avalon.

as Eliot Ness; and *The Twilight Zone*, George Reeves, the former star of *Superman*, died during the summer in an apparent suicide. Forever typecast as "The Man of Steel," Reeves had not been able to find work since the show's cancelation in 1957, although

Sandra Dee finds love in *A Summer Place.*

some have since claimed that he was entertaining several offers at the time of his death, and that (as he left no note) his demise was either due to an accident or foul play. His death remains a mystery.

The Many Loves of Dobie Gillis debuted in the fall, starring Dwayne Hickman as the titular girl-crazy teenager. The character of Dobie's best buddy, Maynard G Krebs was a good indication of how quickly the media had warped and commodified the image of the "beat generation." Instead of being hip, contemplative and creative (à la Kerouac and Ginsberg), Krebs was merely goateed, unwashed and extremely lazy. Coined in 1958 by San Francisco newspaper columnist Herb Caen, the term "beatnik" went into the American lexicon as a connotation for the likes of Krebs, rather than Kerouac's ideal of "a swinging group of new American men intent on joy."

Movie News

Hollywood jumped on the beatnik bandwagon too, releasing Albert Zugsmith's *The Beat Generation* and Roger Corman's *A Bucket of Blood*, a horror-comedy about a coffeehouse busboy whose grisly art projects bring him fame in the world of beats.

Other cheap thrills were available in the form of *Teenagers from Outer Space*, *Attack of the Giant Leeches*, and *The Tingler*, a horror film by William Castle that utilized "**Percepto**"—the theater seats were wired with a mild electric current, so as to actually shock the audience!

Rock Hudson and Doris Day, who starred together in the popular romantic farce **Pillow Talk**, made for an extremely incongruous duo.

Neither were exactly what they seemed: the handsome Hudson, a closeted gay man, was lusted after by millions of American women, while Day, already well into her thirties, was usually depicted as the epitome of virginal innocence. The pair were easily the most popular stars of 1959.

Speaking of virginal innocence, the most popular new face of the year was Sandra Dee, the seventeen-year-old actress who appeared in *Imitation of Life*, *Gidget* and *A Summer Place.*

Suddenly Last Summer, Joseph L Mankiewicz's adaptation of Tennessee Williams' 1958 one-act play, starred Elizabeth Taylor as Katherine Hepburn's allegedly insane niece. In reality, Liz's own life continued to take soap-opera-worthy turns; her engagement (and subsequent wedding) to Eddie Fisher brought howls of outrage from fans who blamed Liz for breaking up Fisher's and Debbie Reynolds' "perfect" marriage.

William Wyler's epic **Ben-Hur**, starring Charlton Heston, swept the Academy Awards, thanks in part to Robert L Surtees' amazing cinematography.

Bell Company

"Phone-booth packing," the art of seeing just how many people you can fit into a phone booth, briefly became the rage on college campuses.

Just-over-the-knee "short" skirts and knitted sweaters were popular with women, with chokers as

a common accessory. Panti-Legs, the first pantyhose, were marketed by North Carolina's Glen Raven Mills.

Barbie dolls, named after the daughter of Mattel Toy Company co-founder Ruth Handler, made their debut at the 1959 New York Toy Fair. Dealer interest was lukewarm at first—Barbie was thought to be a little too, er, "developed" for a young girl's doll—but picked up considerably when Mattel quickly sold out of its initial shipment of five hundred thousand dolls. Barbie, and her endless supply of outfits and accessories, have since become an integral part of life for pre-adolescent American girls.

Zing In The Tail

In its 1960 sales catalog, the Plymouth company reported that—according to University of Detroit wind tunnel tests— "stabilizers" (aka tailfins) "bring the center of pressure back toward the rear" while driving, and that their fins actually reduced the need to make steering corrections in cross winds. Despite such lofty claims, the tailfin was now a shrinking, vanishing species. 1960 Chryslers still offered relatively sharp fins (along with push-button automatictransmission, air conditioning, power windows, and power seats), but many cars, including Oldsmobile's 1960 Super 88 Holiday SceniCoupe ("radiantly fashioned for the Rocketing Sixties"), sported flattened or angled fins. Others, like the 1960 Pontiac Ventura Sports Coupe, got rid of the fins entirely, relying instead on futuristically styled tail-lights for rear-end flashiness.

'59 Barbie-doll purse.

TOP ALBUMS

THE KINGSTON TRIO
The Kingston Trio At Large

HENRY MANCINI
The Music From Peter Gunn

THE KINGSTON TRIO
Here We Go Again!

JOHNNY MATHIS
Heavenly

MARTIN DENNY
Exotica

ACADEMY AWARDS

BEST PICTURE
Ben-Hur
directed by William Wyler

BEST ACTOR
Charlton Heston
Ben-Hur

BEST ACTRESS
Simone Signoret
Room at the Top

Index

Acknowledgements

The publishers would like to thank the following sources for their kind permission to reproduce the pictures in this book:

The Advertising Archives

Corbis-Bettmann/UPI

Everett

Ronald Grant Archive

The Image Bank/Archive Photos

London Features International Ltd

Pictorial Press Limited

Every effort has been made to acknowledge correctly and contact the source and/or copyright holder of each picture, and Carlton Books Limited apologises for any unintentional errors or omissions which will be corrected in future editions of this book.

About the Author

Dan Epstein is an award-winning freelance writer and editor who has contributed to many magazines. Since graduating in Film Studies from Vassar College in New York, he has worked for *Chicago Subnation*, a bi-monthly magazine devoted to the city's popular culture, and for the *Los Angeles Reader*. He has also had his work published in *Guitar Player*, *LA Weekly*, *Mojo*, and *Time Out Guide* to Los Angeles.